Michael For Warfare

Johannes Tefo

Published by Thabang Tefo, 2024.

Also by Johannes Tefo

Family spiritual Warfare Books
Generational Curses And Spiritual Warfare: Spiritual Strategies & Principles Of Victory Against Evil Strongholds
Youth's Guide To Spiritual Warfare
A Women's Guide To Spiritual Warfare

Standalone
Deliver Your Soul From Evil
Overcoming Spirit Of Stagnation
The 24: Prophetic Word For This Season 2024 And Beyond
Michael For Warfare
Territorial Spirits: Overcome Evil Strongholds in Your Life And Take Over Your Community With Strategic Warfare And Winning Prayers
Prayers Against Suicide Spirit
Spiritual Warfare When Enough is Enough
Identity In Christ
Prayers Against Satanic Networks

The Workplace You Need: Spiritual Warfare Prayers That Silence Evil Powers At Your Workplace.

Deliverance From Mind Control: Be Free And Delivered From Every Marine Demons Of Mind Control

Times Getting Hard: Scriptures Of Comfort For Hard Days

Battle In The Sea: How To Tackle Spiritual Warfare And Win The Battle

Freedom: Deliverance Of Souls From Captivity

A Dedicated Prayer Lifestyle: Simple Tips To Effective Prayer Lifestyle

Deliverance From Sexual Dreams

Sexual Lust, Demons, And Impurity

Redefined By Fire: Unleashing The Power Of The Holy Spirit Within.

Table of Contents

Dedicated to the body of Christ, the warriors in Christ.

God bless!

Introduction.

I went through the Bible to find several scriptures that specifically talk about Angel Michael. The only book that has a little bit of content about Angel Michael is the Book of Daniel. To me, it seems like Archangel Michael mostly is found in prophetic books—since Apostle John also had a peak in the future about the showdown between Michael and Lucifer.

I have listed all the scripture references about Michael below.

Daniel 10:13: "But the prince of the kingdom of Persia withstood me one and twenty days: but, lo, Michael, one of the chief princes, came to help me; and I remained there with the kings of Persia."

Daniel 10:21: "But I will shew thee that which is noted in the scripture of truth: and there is none that holdeth with me in these things, but Michael your prince."

Daniel 12:1: "And at that time shall Michael stand up, the great prince which standeth for the children of thy people: and there shall be a time of trouble, such as never was since there was a nation even to that same time: and at that time thy people shall be delivered, every one that shall be found written in the book."

Jude 1:9: "Yet Michael the archangel, when contending with the devil he disputed about the body of Moses, durst not bring against him a railing accusation, but said, The Lord rebuke thee."

Revelation 12:7-9 (NIV): *"Then war broke out in heaven. Michael and his angels fought against the dragon, and the dragon and his angels fought back. But he was not strong enough, and they lost their place in heaven. The great dragon was hurled down—that ancient serpent called the devil, or Satan, who leads the whole world astray. He was hurled to the earth, and his angels with him."*

I have to tell you that, it is quite a long haul to write a whole book with few scriptures like that. However, as I was spiritually inspired to write this book, I remember walking in my yard back and forth about how this book with go about, I then went to the loo. As I was still reminiscing about the content, I had a mini vision of the Host of heaven moving swiftly in the sky passing by my house.

It was a deep confirmation for me to continue with this amazing book. I had designed the cover of the book before I even wrote it. This is how I do it to be inspired as we all know about the hiccups and long-dead author's block for finishing their work.

The vision of the Lord kept me going. And even through the process of writing, I have met this amazing being, Michael, through dreams and visions. However, I don't want to dwell much on dreams and visions.

Though, I have to let it out that, as the prophet of God, God mostly uses dreams and visions to reach to me. As every dream and vision has to be scaled through the Word of God, I am not ashamed that, they come from Almighty God.

This is the time of the outpouring of the spirit of God. Christ is the well of the Living water, which is the spirit of the Living God. The rock of our strength, the strength of our hearts. I decree open heaven over your life as you continue to read this book. Let Michael and his host of heavenly armies guard you and your family in all things.

It is with great pleasure to write this book because Michael is the end-time warrior who will lead us against the wiles of evil. When the term "spiritual warfare" is mentioned, in the spirit realm, Christ the head of the church, has charged Michael and his Angels for spiritual warfare, binding principalities and powers of darkness as we continue to stand on prayer.

This is the end time material to strengthen you. To equip us for the battle ahead. Cheers!

The Warrior Archangel

As you open the pages of this book, you step into a world where the celestial and earthly realms converge. In this realm, you'll encounter the enigmatic and powerful figure known as Archangel Michael. Let's embark on a journey to understand the essence of this warrior archangel, his significance, and the roles he plays in the realm of spiritual warfare.

Imagine a celestial being, majestic and resplendent, his presence evoking a sense of awe and reverence. This is Archangel Michael, a mighty warrior among the angels. You are about to discover his story and the reasons he's regarded as a guardian, protector, and symbol of divine strength.

Michael's name itself carries profound meaning. "Michael" translates to "Who is like God?" This question underscores the archangel's significance. In the scriptures, during a celestial rebellion, when some angels challenged God's authority, Michael courageously led the loyal angelic forces, declaring, "Who is like God?" This became a battle cry and a testament to his unwavering devotion to the Living King.

But what is spiritual warfare, and why does Michael play such a crucial role in it? Spiritual warfare isn't a physical battle, but a struggle between the forces of good and evil, light and darkness. Michael, with his flaming sword and unwavering commitment, is a beacon of hope and protection in this ongoing cosmic battle.

As you delve deeper into this book, you'll come to understand that Archangel Michael is a constant presence in many belief systems and cultures. While he may be most prominent in Christianity, he's also recognized in Judaism, Islam, and various other faiths. This universality emphasizes his significance as a protector and guide to countless souls.

The image of Michael as a warrior may seem intimidating, but he's also a symbol of compassion and divine love. He is often depicted as a protector of the innocent, a shield against the malevolent forces that seek to harm humanity. He stands ready to aid those who call upon him, offering his assistance in times of danger and distress.

In this book, you'll also discover that Archangel Michael's presence extends beyond the grand battles between good and evil. He is a guardian in your daily life, a shield against the trials and tribulations you may encounter. His guidance can help you navigate the challenges you face, both internal and external.

With Michael by your side, you'll learn to recognize the weapons of light that are at your disposal. These include faith, prayer, and the power of positive intention. You don't have to face the darkness alone, for the archangel's radiant presence can help illuminate your path.

I will also introduce you to my stories and real-life testimonies of how I have experienced Michael's divine intervention. You'll be inspired by the encounters of victory in adversity, showing that even in the darkest of times, there is a glimmer of hope.

Archangel Michael is a powerful ally in the realm of spiritual warfare, a steadfast protector, and a symbol of divine strength and compassion. You're about to embark on a remarkable journey, one that explores the celestial and the earthly, and brings you closer to the understanding of an archangel who stands as a beacon of hope and a warrior for all who seek his guidance.

And you will also understand about the role in the end time he will be playing. From Genesis to Revelation, Michael is in a constant celestial battle with Satan. As the children of light, we are on Michael's side as we wage spiritual battles on earth on our knees working with Him.

God is the Lord of the armies. The Lord of Host is His name. and He is the man of war. Warfare is part and parcel of the kingdom of God. And we always thrive because greater is He who is in us than he who is in the world.

War in heaven.

It's Michael and his angels' vs the dragon and his angels. This statement makes Michael and Satan of superior nature compared to other celestial bodies. The cause of nature itself felt a deep impact by the fall of Lucifer. It is of great interest that the first war started in the heavenly.

And there is no mention of Christ because Lucifer is billions of times not near to Christ. We usually make mistakes as the body of Christ assuming that it's Christ vs Satan. Christ is the great king. The fight is between the prince vs the prince. Satan is the prince of the power of the air. Michael is the great prince who stands on behalf of the nation of Israel.

Daniel 12:1: "And at that time shall Michael stand up, the great prince which standeth for the children of thy people: and there shall be a time of trouble, such as never was since there was a nation even to that same time: and at that time thy people shall be delivered, every one that shall be found written in the book."

I strongly believe Satan is contending with Michael against the nation of Israel to turn it into destruction. He destroyed the line of Adam with a serpentine seed of evil—from the time of Adam till now, human beings have been at their knees fighting with the forces of evil. Throughout the history of the people of God, Michael has been the pillar of strength during difficult times.

He is only mentioned 4 times in the bible. But since Satan has been killing, stealing, and destroying, Michael has been defending, fighting, and protecting the people of God. We cannot see the fight with our naked eyes but if we can remember how many times we have been spared destruction, the hand of the Lord of Host was at work.

Moses' generation knew Him as the Man of War. As believers and followers of Christ, we are the army of God on this earth. And we have the heavenly army that is not against us but for us. And Archangel Michael and his hosts are one of those who are for us. I pray that we walk in a renewed mind so that we can see the mighty arm of the Lord in these last days. There is a lot happening in the spirit realm. Things are shaking and shifting—paving the way for the king. Faith in the Most High God will unlock all the doors that have shut.

The most spiritual assets you have are your eyes, ears, and mind. These are spiritual portals the holy spirit uses to reach you. Spiritual visions and dreams play out in your mind—what we call mental images. This happens when your mind is renewed by the Holy Spirit. it is vital for brothers and sisters to renew their minds through the power of the Word and Spirit of God.

Romans 12:1 *Therefore, I urge you, brothers and sisters, in view of God's mercy, to offer your bodies as a living sacrifice, holy and pleasing to God—this is your true and proper worship.*

²Do not conform to the pattern of this world, but be transformed by the renewing of your mind. Then you will be able to test and approve what God's will is—his good, pleasing and perfect will.

As the body of Christ, we usually talk about how the spirit of discernment is a powerful gift. You will be double-minded trying to discern spirits while conformed to the pattern of this word in your mind. As a warrior in Christ, you will need all the weapons of God when contending with evil forces.

We are contending with the enemy around the clock. There is no break, or come tomorrow when you are dealing with forces of darkness. We are live soldiers in the jungle—you never know what might happen. But by faith, we will always be the lions that conquer.

Apostle Paul invites us to the real spiritual fight through the book of Ephesians. These are the principalities and powers of darkness Moses was dealing with in Egypt while delivering the Children of Israel with the mighty Rod of God. The mystery was in the River Nile where marine powers and strongholds reside. We cannot also forget the prophet Daniel who was up against the Princes of Babylon. These princes and princesses are spirits.

If Christians could approach spiritual warfare from the heavenly perspective, we would be victorious at all times. It would make all the difference by seeing yourself in high places with Christ waging war. And we will also have a bird's-eye view of what is happening in the spirit realm, knowing the territorial powers of certain regions and engaging in a strategic spiritual battle that results in victory.

Satan has millions of strategies. Sadly, this is what the Lord revealed to me in spirit. we are also armed with deadlier weapons over the kingdom of darkness. We must become the enemy of the kingdom of darkness. The kingdom of darkness must be troubled. It is written that since the time of John the Baptist, the kingdom of God has suffered violence.

This can happen when we can utilize the God-given authority in our lives. The authority to bind and lose, the authority of the name, the blood of Jesus, the Word of God, the power of praise and worship, and many more. I have also noticed that heartfelt prayers are the key to the heart of God.

David was the man after God's own heart. He always wanted what was best for God. The man, David, would not sleep or wink his eyes until the ark of the Lord was resting in the Holy place. Though it was King Solomon who built the temple. However, his devotion to his God was extraordinary. The love of God is the first among all things. David teaches us about faith, love, and hope in the God of Jacob.

As we are talking about war in heaven, it shows you that nice prayers and a nice Christian life wouldn't do much to the kingdom of darkness. Satan comes to steal, kill, and destroy. When there is an absence of God in someone's life, there is bound to be destruction. It is evident even to the fallen angels that fell by sleeping with women, who are now principal demons, that there is no love in them and hate humankind to the core.

I recall one night I was praising and worshipping God, then I had a vision after I went to sleep, I saw Azazel in spirit—the fallen angel that taught men war bringing destruction upon the world. The way I was worshipping, he said, he recalled the time he was in third heaven praising God. It shows you that angels also have emotion and remorse like humans. The book of Enoch has detailed information about these watchers who made a vow to sleep with women.

In the retelling of the story of the sons of God and daughters of men (Gen. 6:1–4) in the First Book of Enoch, Azazel is one of the leaders of the angels who desired the daughters of men (6:4), and it was he who taught human beings how to manufacture weapons and ornaments (8:1–2).

The identification of this Azazel with the biblical Azazel is clear from the continuation of the story, as the angel Raphael is commanded to "bind the hands and feet of Azazel and cast him into the darkness. Make an opening to the wilderness which is in Dudael and cast him there. Put upon him hard sharp rocks" (10:4–5). In

The character of Azazel as a fallen angel is found in the book of Enoch. The book of Enoch is not part of the Bible and part of the Apocrypha.

In the book of Enoch, Azazel is a fallen angel. He is a leader of other fallen angels and responsible for evil in the world. He has led so much destruction that the book encourages Jewish readers to ascribe all sin to him.

In the Apocrypha, Azazel is a leader of rebellious angels, as seen in the Book of Enoch. He leads the pre-Flood civilizations of men, and giants (perhaps Nephilim), in all matters of warfare and witchcraft.

It is worth noting that God allowed His Holy angels like Michael and others to bind Azazel to the underworld in a desolate place until the day of Judgement of hell fire. Many scholars believe he is a desert demon according to Levictus 16. We see the hand of God at work through Archangel Michael even before humankind. We do not have a record of the event before the creation of the first man, Adam. But the fall of Satan happened before humans.

Without a doubt, I believe it was Angel Michael who dethroned Lucifer from his position. The name Michael means "who is like God?" or "gift from God." I can literally flip it like "Who is like God" dethroned who wanted to be like God. Ezekiel 28 and Isaiah 14 it's an interesting chapters to discover the motive of Lucifer and his fall from grace.

I have had a few encounters with the devil. The devil is not what many assume him to be. Hollywood has twisted our minds and has robbed us of the reality of who Satan is. He transforms into the angel of light if he wants to deceive many. Isaiah 14 and Ezekiel 28 say he committed many sins because of his trade. Trade is a business term—and that would make the devil the great negotiator in business as he had to deceive millions of angels to follow him. He is the negotiator of the souls of men and women. Those who went on to open themselves up to him offered them fame, wealth, power, and riches. This is what he also wanted to offer to Christ—the son of the Living God.

"You were the seal of perfection" "Full of wisdom and perfect in beauty" This is Lucifer. The gift of God are without repentance. The devil is the most beautiful Angel to ever be created and is full of wisdom that is still using even today to manipulate us and deceive us from the Godly path of God. When he appears to you he appears as the angel of light. He would never let you see his state after the fall.

The fall of Lucifer brought nothing but destruction to the universe that we see and that we cannot see. First of all, we are dealing with a spiritual being highly ranked that used to walk in the presence of God. It can only be through the blood of Jesus Christ that we are able to conquer the evil powers directed at us as flying arrows from the kingdom of the devil.

I am not in any way glorifying the devil but allowing you to see the reality so that you can be the warrior in Christ who knows both worlds. Because you cannot fight what you do not know and expect to be victorious. Moses was trained in Egypt so that he could be the perfect fit to be the great deliverer he was. He had to see the stronghold of Pharaoh—the strengths and weaknesses so that he could defeat him. You had to be bold like Moses to go to Pharaoh.

Pharaoh was worshipped as a deity in those days. Other nations bowed to the Egyptian empire. Moses had to contend with high-ranking witches and wizards of Egypt who were professionals and professors when it came to divination, sorcery, astrology, necromancy, and witchcraft.

Walking with God requires you to be bold like a lion. Boldness is an act of faith. We can learn a lot from people of faith in the bible like Moses, Elijah, and Enoch. We have to learn that life is spiritual. Elisha was not moved by the army that besieged him—he was well rounded with life in the spirit that he saw spiritual protection for him—the mighty angelic army of God surrounding him.

We have the Archangel—the prince of believers who would not let any plague come near us. He has always been a contenting warrior for ages. I strongly believe he was responsible for the deliverance of Israel from Egypt. And also the time they were coming from Babylon as captives.

Even to this day, Michael the Prince still has responsibility for great issues concerning Israel and the world at large. It is written in Daniel 12 that in these last days, Michael shall arise. When Michael arises, just know that Israel is about to take center stage in the world.

Daniel 12:1*: "And at that time shall Michael stand up, the great prince which standeth for the children of thy people: and there shall be a time of trouble, such as never was since there was a nation even to that same time: and at that time thy people shall be delivered, every one that shall be found written in the book."*

The great prince stands for the believers whose names are written in the Book of Life. Psalm 91 says "He shall give angels charge over you to keep you". The term "Angels" means many. It literally means you will have the heavenly arm or host that is for you and protecting you against evil forces you do not see with your naked eyes. Because angels are ministering spirits—you see them with your spiritual eyes.

Warfare is in the heavenly places. Strategic prophets like Daniel and Ezekiel knew that if they wanted to change the system of the course of their lives and nations, they had to engage the heavenly in prayer. As a child, I used to see angels descending from Heaven and going to different places. I was always fascinated by those dreams and visions.

Many prophetic individuals also see clouds in their dreams often—bright clouds and dark clouds. Bright clouds represent the glory of God. I learned that whenever I pray in spirit when I see dark clouds, it represents an evil stronghold over the region. I wrote a book about territorial spirits. Many of you are fighting territorial spirits unaware. Some of the breakthroughs that you dare of, need you to break evil forces within your regions.

It was revealed in my spirit to wage warfare in a strategic way. Strategic ways mean you go after the kings, not lesser powers. If you can dethrone the king, you have won the victory. It would not do you any good, shouting to demons while they are being strengthened in high places by principalities and powers. You have to bind powerful spirits in the realm of the heavenly—cutting their power supply before you cast out demons.

Demons are the lowest rank in the kingdom of Satan. We should study the enemy if we are to see great deliverance and victory in the kingdom of God. I have seen souls of great men and women of God being caged and bound in the second heaven—the highest kingdom of Satan. Even in the marine kingdom, the underwater realm, the lives of many people are manipulated and destinies are destroyed.

We should learn about the mystery of drying up the evil rivers and binding and loosing, applying, and pleading the blood of Jesus to restrict the stubborn powers of the enemy. We have so many weapons of warfare, and powerful ones to dismantle the forces of evil that we do not see with our naked eyes. Being moved by faith will make you see things you wouldn't normally see.

The Word says "Let the weak say I am strong, and let the strong say I am weak", declare that you see in spirit even if you don't. declare who God says you are. Declare what the scriptures of God say about you. Authority and power of God come through your mouth. The power is vested in your tongue to move mountains. To shake nations with your words. The same commission that was given to Jeremiah, is the same call of authority for believers.

The battle is on. And the battle is in the air. The nations of God have to know about these powers that have been hindering the prayers of saints from arising like a cloud of smoke and fire to the very throne of God. This is the mystery that the prophet Daniel knew. The second heaven is that place of power of darkness that is in constant battle with believers. Many souls are caged in this prison place by principalities.

HALF OF THE ADVANCED technology that comes up this day are manufactured in this kingdom. I have the first hand of witnessing these things. High places, second heaven, marine world, and other strange places of dominion that hunt the souls of men and women for destruction. He comes to steal, kill, and destroy. There is no love in his kingdom.

Stay strong in the Lord of Glory. Our God is the God of all power and glory, the Holy and the Mighty One. Submit yourself to God, and resists him by worshipping and praising the one who is worthy to be praised and blessed—God the Father and Christ Jesus, the Lord, our savior.

The presence of Michael.

When Prince Michael is around the corner, there is peace and a sense of God's love and protection over your life. You sense the presence of God through a scent of perfection. Prophetic people usually see mini visions of light flashing over their eyes or mental impressions of the Divine presence.

When you know you know. It is the act of supernatural knowing that comes from the gift of word of knowledge and wisdom. I personally, see vision in my mind when the Divine presence of Michael is around. I have mastered the art of listening in spirit—it would be confirmed in my heart that the mighty Angel of the Most High is around the corner. Sometimes Angels just appear and stare at you and say nothing. They do not talk that much. Psalm 103 says they harken unto the voice of the Lord and excel in strength.

As a child of God, you have the Holy Spirit in you that reveals all things to you. It is in your ability through faith to tap into the gifts of the spirit to see the wonders of God. It is not God's problem if you cannot hear and see in the spirit because we are blessed with all spiritual blessings in the heavenly places in Christ.

It takes a sacrifice of the flesh to walk in the spirit. it is the best decision you can make for yourself. I invite you to walk in the power and authority of God by walking not in sight but by faith. It is by faith that we are able to walk with God. Same with Angels, it is through faith in Christ that we can boldly claim our inheritance and spiritual heritage, and walk as Abraham walked.

Abraham walked with Angels. Abraham ate with Angels. Abraham was a friend of God. When you are friends with someone, you talk with them, commune with them, appreciate them and honor them. We can do the same with God. When you have a deep fellowship with God, you have a deep fellowship with Angels. Angels walks in humility and reverence before God. The secret to elevation in spirit is through humility and devotion. David humbled himself through fasting.

As we continue to pray and fast, seeking the face of the Most High, we shall behold the glory of God like Moses. Moses came from the mountain shining like an Angel of the Lord. Every time he went to the tabernacle of the Lord, he came back as a different person. This happens when you spend quality time in the secret place with the God of the Universe, who shall reveal Christ unto us.

It amazes me that in heaven there are angels who are assigned to worship God timelessly.

Isaiah 6: 1-3 In the year that king Uzziah died I saw also the LORD sitting upon a throne, high and lifted up, and his train filled the temple.

2 Above it stood the seraphims: each one had six wings; with twain he

covered his face, and with twain he covered his feet, and with twain he did fly.

3 And one cried unto another, and said, Holy, holy, holy, is the LORD of

hosts: the whole earth is full of his glory.

These seraphims have been saying "Holy, Holy, Holy," since the beginning of times. We will also experience the fullness of the glory of God while on earth if we can worship and praise. We enter into His presence with thanksgiving and into the gates with praise. God is the great king.

Psalm 100:4 Enter into his gates with thanksgiving, and into his courts with praise: be

thankful unto him, and bless his name.

This is the ultimate way of getting into the presence of God effortlessly. By praising and worshipping the Creator of the universe. I am stressing this part of getting into the presence of God because you will develop spiritual senses when you constantly appear before the great light of God. You would never be the same when you constantly live in His glory. Wisdom, understanding and knowledge comes down flowing from those who appear before the face of the Lord. He says come boldly to the throne of grace and ask for mercy.

Hebrews 10:19-22 Having therefore, brethren, boldness to enter into the holiest by the blood of Jesus,

20 By a new and living way, which he hath consecrated for us, through the veil, that is to say, his flesh;

21 And having an high priest over the house of God;

22 Let us draw near with a true heart in full assurance of faith, having our

hearts sprinkled from an evil conscience, and our bodies washed with pure

water.

WE HAVE BOLDNESS BECAUSE we are righteous. Abraham was counted for righteous for believing in God. By the same believe in God, we are also counted righteous. We are called the children of God born through the power of the Spirit of God—preceded from Christ. Self-righteous has nothing to do with the righteousness that comes from God.

Prophet Isaiah foretold about the robe of righteousness and the garment of praise. These are the gifts of God to them that believe in the death of the Cross and resurrection of Jesus Christ, the Son of the Living God.

When we ascend on high in spirit, we a going up to the heavenly Jerusalem, the city of God. The city builds by the Word of God. Where Christ is well- known as the Word. Where there are millions of Angels and redeemed Saints praising their king, the Almighty God. In this place, we tap into the glory and the power of God, our face beholds the glory of God so that we many never grow weary in faith.

Revelation 19:11 And I saw heaven opened, and behold a white horse; and he that sat upon him was called Faithful and True, and in righteousness he doth judge and make

war.

12 His eyes were as a flame of fire, and on his head were many crowns; and

he had a name written, that no man knew, but he himself.

13 And he was clothed with a vesture dipped in blood: and his name is

called The Word of God.

I have met Archangel Michael in spirit, I will go in detail in the next chapter. Though, when Michael is around, you feel at peace and protected. He usually like wearing purple or blue outfit. I believe it is his Angelic color. As He is a warrior Angel, He always has a huge sword in His hand.

He is the defender of the believers and non-believers alike. There are account of non-believers who had an encounter with Michael who also went on to be saved. There is joy in heaven when believers come to Christ. Before writing this book, I read various books that talk about Archangel Michael, and most of them talk about how to summon Michael and prayers to Michael.

As someone who is rooted in the Word, it is a good thing to honor Angels as they are always in the presence of God. But we do not pray to Angels but to the Most High God. We worship the Most High God.

Revelation 19:10 And I fell at his feet to worship him. And he said unto me, See thou do it not: I am thy fellowservant, and of thy brethren that have the testimony of Jesus:

worship God: for the testimony of Jesus is the spirit of prophecy.

Revelation 19: 20 Bless the LORD, ye his angels, that excel in strength, that do his

commandments, hearkening unto the voice of his word.

Angels listens to the voice of God to perform His will. Angel Michael is under the direction of Christ and the Holy Spirit. we pray unto our Father in the name of Jesus Christ to dispatch mighty Angels like Michael to take charge over us in times of trouble. When we sense danger we can ask the Lord of Armies to dispatch the warriors of heaven for our sake. God is omniscient, omnipotent and omnipresence.

He even hears our deepest thoughts. In a blink of an eye, He can even answer your thoughts without you lifting your mouth. He listens to silent prayers. He knows you more than you do.

Psalm 147:4 He telleth the number of the stars; he calleth them all by their names.

5 Great is our Lord, and of great power: his understanding is infinite.

Psalm 139: 1 O lord, thou hast searched me, and known me.

2 Thou knowest my downsitting and mine uprising, thou understandest my

thought afar off.

I included these two verse to complement the greatness of the Lord. Who is infinite in all things. Who cannot be comprehended by our mere minds. We are thankful of the Holy Spirit indwelling our bodies that reveal to us the mystery of heavens.

As I conclude this chapter, the same way you feel when the Holy Spirit of God is upon you, is the same way you feel when there is the presence of Michael. Michael represents everything that has to do with the will of God. We are to move in spirit if we're to walk with angels. Jesus Christ stressed faith in His ministry. It is still through faith at this day and age, if you want to mount up with heavenly wings and fly above. God bless you.

My Personal encounter with Michael.

Let me start by saying, I grew up in a South African village called Mashashane. It is one of the most feared villages in the region for witchcraft. In fact, if you ever travel to South African, you will hear about the province where I am from as the cornerstone of witchcraft practices. Anyway, witchcraft is widespread in Africa and beyond. So as a Christian believer, my view of how the enemy operate with always be different from the western believe.

Because where I am from we do not hear about witchcraft but see it with our own eyes. The village has molded me into being the prayer warrior I am today. You will always see the emphasis of prayer in my writing. Especially spiritual warfare, which I believe many are starting to be woken to the reality that life is spiritual.

From an early age, my eyes have always been opened to the spiritual world. I used to see angels, demons and agents of the Devil in spirit even before I became a staunch believer. Parents always stressed prayer before sleep. My grandmother when she was around—she would call me at midnight to pray. She always knew that this is the time whereby witches and wizards meet to perform their demonic assignments.

Not that we were leaving in fear of the Devil, no. men and women ought to meet with God in their secret place as they commitment and devotion to their God. It started with prayer then we started fasting, and reading the Word of God. This is the roadmap of a serious spiritual journey. He says come with thanksgiving and praise in my court.

The gates of God open when we offer thanksgiving. But the journey does not stop there. We get to the courtroom of God through praise.

Psalm 100: 4 Enter into his gates with thanksgiving, and into his courts with praise: be thankful unto him, and bless his name.

This verse has been the pillar if my life. I knew that this verse entails the gateway to the heart of God. The gate way to the glory of God. David was a man after God's heart because he placed the act of praise above all things. What you worship and what you praise control you. The spirit of God what at move in David. That even after he committed adultery and murder, he pleaded with God to not remove Holy Spirit in him and upon him.

There are two places where you find the term 'Holy Spirit' in the old testament. In Psalm 51:11 and Isaiah 63:10. Although there are different instances of the works of the holy spirit. Here I am referring to the term "Holy Spirit" which popularly known in the new testament especially in the Acts of Apostles.

The reason why I am emphasizing prayer, fasting, praise and worship is that, these principles of the kingdom has opened my eyes to the spirit world where you meet celestial bodies and the divine. Jesus Christ speaks at all times, whether we hear or miss it, He speaks. I have met his through series of dreams and visions. I am in the prophetic office by the call of God, as a prophetic it is vital to be sensitive to the spirit of world.

This is where the spirit of discerning comes in. To be able to discern between good and evil. The renewed mind of Christ will always know the perfect will of God. There are some brothers and sisters who were fooled by the Angels of the Devil masquerading as the Angels of light. I don't know anyone who has ever met a horned-red Devil in dreams or visions.

The enemy will appear pleasing. You will always see this beautiful mermaid televised on Hollywood. The world will make Satan to look innocent and make God evil. This is the generation that celebrate evil as Holy and Holy as evil. We have come to that. So brothers and sisters, the enemy would not trick you or manipulate you if it looks phony and ugly.

Satan is the most handsome dude ever. Almost all fallen and demons shapeshift to glorious state when they want to deceive the world. Therefore, do not neglect the free spiritual gifts Christ has died for on the Cross. We are spiritually blessed in High places in Christ. Note that, these evil powers also have strongholds in high places. But you are far above them because Christ dwells in the highest of the heavens to date, which is the third heaven.

We meet Angelic powers like Michael and Gabriel because we are in Christ. Even Moses the great man of God, saw Jesus Christ in spirit. I actually received the revelation that all prophets of God in the bible, had an encounter with the Father and Christ. Adam as the first man, it would be revealed that there will be a second Adam.

It was God in the garden of Eden who clothed Adam and Eve after deception. The blood of Animal was wearing were from Lambs. The blood of the Lamb was shed in the garden. The garden of Eden is the face of God. It literally means that to meet God, you have to go through the process of Blood. Abraham also, after Mount Moriah sacrifice, he went on have a deeper relationship with God like never before.

There is power in the blood of the Lamb. All the Angels of God point us to deeper relationship with the God of the universe. Any Angel that doesn't lead you to Almighty God is a false one. Michael the prince, is the warrior commander of the Heavenly Armies under the leadership of God and Christ. All Angels listens and performs the Word of God.

Angels are very powerful. You cannot retain strength if one of them walk in your room right now. Angels were created from fire. They are minster of fire. Even swords they carry flames with fire of the glory of God. What's more, they live in the presence of God where is fiery.

I always do wage warfare for my village—pleading the blood of Jesus over my community and interceding on behalf of my people to come to Christ. I did not know that all along Angel Michal was dispatched to assist me over my community. In spirit I will see the bright clouds over my community after spiritual warfare. I would see principal demons and fallen ones leave the area after an intense battle. Bear in mind that, this is a once off thing.

Many would say it is not scriptural to wage warfare in the heavenly. If you are a strategic prophet, you will see the need to wage good warfare for your community or city like Prophet Daniel did. Prophet Daniel through territorial warfare was able to foster and change the future of Israel. Knowing the truth will make us stand on the truth. When he learned from the book of Jeremiah the Prophet that it would take 70 years of captivity, he went to his knees and reasoned with the Most High.

He was allowed to see the future Messiah and the end of the world. I believe some of the information he was not allowed to share. It was information sealed for the wise. Every now and then, man and women must stand up in their faith to wage warfare for their community because this is what the agents of Satan do. They fight for the territory of cities, town and villages, they occupy over these regions if Christian are not in prayer and unity in faith.

For every territorial warfare, Archangel Michael arises. Where there is prince of Persia, Michael is there. Where there is Satan, Michael is there. Michael is the prince over believers and over those that fears the Lord. The fear of the Lord is the beginning of all beautiful things. All things come from sincere reverend of the Mighy King.

Hebrews 1:14 Are they not all ministering spirits, sent forth to minister for them who shall be heirs of salvation?

He gives Angels charge over us, to protect us and defend us against the wiles of the enemy.

Psalm 34: 7 The angel of the LORD encampeth round about them that fear him, and delivereth them.

Psalm 35: 5 Let them be as chaff before the wind: and let the angel of the LORD chase them.

Psalm 91: 11 For he shall give his angels charge over thee, to keep thee in all thy ways. 12 They shall bear thee up in their hands, lest thou dash thy foot against a stone.

Satan quoted this line while tempting Jesus. Throughout history people of faith have been using Psalms 91 as their protective charm against the wiles of the Devil. For Satan to quotes it, it means it's a powerful protective Psalm. I have seen the power of God while using this Psalm, meditating on it, praying it and acting on it. Jesus Christ is the secret place of the Most High. He is the highest priest in the kingdom of God who opened the veil of His body so that we can experience the Divine presence of the MOST HIGH GOD.

In the book of Ephesians 2:6 we are seated with Christ in the heavenly places. We all know that Jesus Christ is in paradise in the 3rd heaven. The secret place is a spiritual place not a physical place. It is in Christ who seated in the right hand of the Mighty Father. This is the place of POWER. Man and women of God draws powers and authority from this glorified place of light.

The moment of writing this piece, I went outside to relieve myself. In villages we have outside toilets unlike in towns. As I came outside, I was Host of heaven (Angels) moving to a different direction in the sky. My eyes were open in spirit to see this beautiful vision. I believe it was a confirmation for me to continue writing this book.

Because I always had that desire and sensation to write a book about Angels since many do not have deep knowledge of these celestial bodies. I had only few encounters that I can include, but would not make a full print. I did a thorough research, then I stopped.

A thing about me, I write when I am inspired by the Spirit of God. Today I am truly inspired to write this piece of work to you.

Okay, my personal encounter with Michael happened in spirit, in spirit I mean an out-of-body experience where I felt where I was fighting demons in the sky over my region but outer space. There a kingdoms and government of evil forces in the heavenly places. Apostle Paul wrote about these powers in Ephesians 6:12—principalities and powers of evil.

To really establish the government of God in your home or city, you have to go extra mile. Destined people are separated from the world. You would have to be separated like Elijah and John the Baptist. You are able to receive serious divine revelation and knowledge when you are in the wilderness alone. Sadly, many do not want to take the narrow road. The narrow road is the way to home.

Looking at prophets and Apostles in the bible, they had distinct lifestyle of prayer. They were into the ministry of the Word and Prayer. By prayer, I mean all kinds of prayers. As we are advised to pray all kinds of prayers in the book of Ephesians.

Every human being has guardian angel since from birth. However, those called by God have special armies waiting to lead them into their destiny. There are different kinds of angels with different tasks. Michael is widely known for defending the people of Israel and believers in general in all walks of life. Prophets and Apostle mostly encounter this angelic force since He is a spiritual warfare warrior.

When Michael arises, there come victory. He never loses a battle. He demoted Lucifer from heaven. He will still in future chain him and throw him in the eternal damnation reserved for fallen angels as it is written about him.

Revelation 20: 1-2 And I saw an angel come down from heaven, having the key of the bottomless pit and a great chain in his hand. 2 And he laid hold on the dragon, that old serpent, which is the Devil, and Satan, and bound him a thousand years,

The prophetic army of God its defender is Angel Michael and His angels. He was with Moses in Egypt. And led him to victory. He was with Samuel, Gideon, Barak, David, Jehoshaphat, Apostles and more.

Even today, He is still with us. Fighting principalities and powers warring with believers each day. When Archangel Michael is around fear goes, peace reigns. When you are propelled to decree and declare in spirit, know that the angels are around.

I have had a deep experience with Michael during my warfare seasons with evil forces and powers of the sky. There is a level that one reach when all hell have been tempering with your destiny in your life. Those who goes through rough seasons in life are destined for greatness. We are all destined for greatness. But they are those with special assignments like caliber of Elijah, John the Baptist, Jeremiah, Jesus Christ etc.

I believe you are also one of the special warrior for the end time season to wage war to the kingdom of darkness through your faith. Faith is paramount. Faith is the key. Faith is everything. Keep the faith and keep going till the end of time. No weapon formed against you shall prosper. It's only a matter of time that you shall be elevated and mount up with wings and fly.

There a horses of fire in heaven waiting for you. These are the horses of the end time warfare. Where at that day Christ will be the king from sea to sea, border to border, from sun rising to sun going down. For years I have been seeing this vision—horses riding swiftly coming through the white clouds—Christ wearing the crown, red apparel followed by tenth of thousands of holy ones.

Revelation 19:11 And I saw heaven opened, and behold a white horse; and he that sat upon him was called Faithful and True, and in righteousness he doth judge and make war. 12 His eyes were as a flame of fire, and on his head were many crowns; and he had a name written, that no man knew, but he himself. 13 And he was clothed with a vesture dipped in blood: and his name is called The Word of God. 14 And the armies which were in heaven followed him upon white horses, clothed in fine linen, white and clean. 15 And out of his mouth goeth a sharp sword, that with it he should smite the nations: and he shall rule them with a rod of iron: and he treadeth the winepress of the fierceness and wrath of Almighty God. 16 And he hath on his vesture and on his thigh a name written, KING OF KINGS, AND LORD OF LORDS.

Jude 1: 14 And Enoch also, the seventh from Adam, prophesied of these, saying, Behold, the Lord cometh with ten thousands of his saints, 15 To execute judgment upon all, and to convince all that are ungodly among them of all their ungodly deeds which they have ungodly committed, and of all their hard speeches which ungodly sinners have spoken against him.

I always say the time we are in are the most important timeline in history. All the prophecy of the ancient biblical prophet's point to these days. As it was in the days of Noah, so shall it be in our days. Even though we do not know the day or the hour, but signs speaks loud. It is a set time to walk in the spirit of God. To exercise walking in faith more and more. God bless.

History of Archangel Michael and Lucifer

The historical battle between Lucifer, also known as Satan or the Devil, and the Archangel Michael is a pivotal event in Christian theology, though it's important to note that the Bible does not provide an extensive narrative of this encounter. Instead, the story is derived from various passages and interpretations found throughout the Bible.

In the past, according to the Bible, Lucifer was a high-ranking angel who rebelled against God's authority. The prophet Isaiah provides one of the key references in Isaiah 14:12-15:

"How art thou fallen from heaven, O Lucifer, son of the morning! how art thou cut down to the ground, which didst weaken the nations! For thou hast said in thine heart, I will ascend into heaven, I will exalt my throne above the stars of God: I will sit also upon the mount of the congregation, in the sides of the north: I will ascend above the heights of the clouds; I will be like the most High. Yet thou shalt be brought down to hell, to the sides of the pit."

This passage is often interpreted as describing Lucifer's pride and rebellion, which led to his fall from grace and his desire to exalt himself above God.

The Archangel Michael is prominently mentioned in the Bible as a powerful and loyal servant of God. In the book of Jude, verse 9, we read: "Yet Michael the archangel, when contending with the devil he disputed about the body of Moses, durst not bring against him a railing accusation, but said, The Lord rebuke thee." This verse portrays Michael's role as a defender of God's will and a powerful adversary against the Devil.

In the present, believers often interpret the ongoing spiritual battle between Lucifer and Michael as a reflection of the struggle between good and evil. In Ephesians 6:12, the apostle Paul warns, "For we wrestle not against flesh and blood, but against principalities, against powers, against the rulers of the darkness of this world, against spiritual wickedness in high places." This verse underscores the idea that the battle is not merely a historical event but an ongoing spiritual struggle faced by all believers.

Regarding the future, the Bible contains prophecies that suggest a culmination of this cosmic battle in the end times. In the Book of Revelation, often seen as a vision of the future, there are references to a final conflict between the forces of evil and the forces of God. Revelation 12:7-9 describes this future battle: "And there was war in heaven: Michael and his angels fought against the dragon; and the dragon fought and his angels, and prevailed not; neither was their place found any more in heaven."

This passage alludes to a future showdown where Michael, the faithful archangel, will lead the celestial forces against Lucifer, the dragon, and his followers. This final confrontation will result in the ultimate victory of good over evil.

Believers are often reminded that we are living in the end times through various prophecies and signs, such as the increase in moral decay, wars, and natural disasters, all mentioned in the Bible (Matthew 24:6-8). It's a call to remain steadfast in one's faith, to be vigilant, and to trust in God's ultimate plan.

In conclusion, the historical fight between Lucifer and the Archangel Michael is a central theme in Christian theology, with references to this cosmic battle found throughout the Bible. The past rebellion, the present spiritual struggle, and the future apocalyptic showdown between good and evil all serve as powerful reminders of the ongoing significance of this theological narrative, emphasizing the need for believers to stay strong in their faith and remain prepared for the end times.

Throughout the Bible, the conflict between Lucifer and Michael is a constant reminder of the ongoing spiritual warfare that Christians face. In 2 Corinthians 10:4, the apostle Paul writes, "For the weapons of our warfare are not carnal but mighty through God to the pulling down of strongholds." This verse emphasizes the need for believers to be armed with spiritual weapons to combat the forces of darkness.

Ephesians 6:11-12 further instructs believers to "put on the whole armor of God" to withstand the wiles of the devil, highlighting the present necessity for spiritual preparedness. This armor includes the belt of truth, the breastplate of righteousness, the shield of faith, the helmet of salvation, and the sword of the Spirit, which is the Word of God. Such symbolism is a reminder that the battle against evil is not just a historical event but an ongoing, daily challenge.

The Archangel Michael, as a powerful defender of God's divine will, serves as an example for believers to emulate. Jude 1:9 emphasizes the importance of respecting the spiritual authority and not slandering the devil but instead invoking the Lord's rebuke. This attitude of reverence for God's authority and trust in His power is essential in facing the challenges of the present.

Moreover, the struggle against evil is not just a cosmic conflict but is also manifest in our daily lives. In 1 Peter 5:8, believers are warned to "be sober, be vigilant; because your adversary the devil, as a roaring lion, walketh about, seeking whom he may devour." This serves as a reminder that the battle is not limited to grand cosmic events but is an ever-present threat that requires constant watchfulness.

Believers are encouraged to stand firm in their faith and remain steadfast in their commitment to righteousness. The biblical narrative of the battle between Lucifer and Michael is a timeless story that reminds us of the importance of being vigilant, prepared, and reliant on God's strength to resist the temptations and challenges that confront us daily.

In conclusion, the story of the battle between Lucifer and the Archangel Michael is not just a historical event or a future prophecy. It is a constant reminder that the struggle between good and evil is a daily reality for believers. The biblical passages that speak of this conflict serve as an exhortation to remain steadfast, vigilant, and equipped with the armor of God to face the spiritual challenges of the present and remain faithful to the divine will.

Who is Prince Michael?

Saint Michael is an archangel, a spiritual warrior in the battle of good versus evil. He is the champion of justice, a healer of the sick, and the guardian of the Church. In art, Saint Michael is always depicted with a sword, a banner, or scales, and is often shown vanquishing Satan in the form of a dragon.

I have to agree that we don't have a lot of information about the celestial bodies. And when God trust you with vision, you will only get a fraction. We know in part; we see in part. Many know Michael as the warrior Angel who restore peace, righteousness by banishing the evil forces that comes through Satan and his host of Angels with motive for destruction.

I have contacted the book of Enoch for more information. I know it is not part of the canon bible. At first I was hesitated to quote it as it gets controversial within the Christian community if you even mention it. It was through revelation that I started treating the book as the Holy book from the Holy ancient prophet of God who saw deep divine mysteries of the then world and the world to come.

What's more? Jude referenced the book of Enoch. I believe Jesus Christ treated it as such. Apostle John also saw the same vision Enoch saw of the end time second coming of Jesus Christ.

Revelation 19:11 And I saw heaven opened, and behold a white horse; and he that sat upon him was called Faithful and True, and in righteousness he doth judge and make war. 12 His eyes were as a flame of fire, and on his head were many crowns; and he had a name written, that no man knew, but he himself. 13 And he was clothed with a vesture dipped in blood: and his name is called The Word of God. 14 And the armies which were in heaven followed him upon white horses, clothed in fine linen, white and clean. 15 And out of his mouth goeth a sharp sword, that with it he should smite the nations: and he shall rule them with a rod of iron: and he treadeth the winepress of the fierceness and wrath of Almighty God. 16 And he hath on his vesture and on his thigh a name written, KING OF KINGS, AND LORD OF LORDS.

Book of Enoch 1:3

1: 3On the account of the elect, the great

Holy One, the God of the world, will

come forth from His dwelling and 4tread

upon the earth,[ii] appearing with His

host in the strength of His might from the

heavens.

This is Jude quoting Enoch;

Jude 1:9

"9Behold! He comes with ten

thousands of His holy ones to

execute judgment upon all, to

destroy all the ungodly, to convict

all flesh of all the works of their

ungodliness which they have

ungodly committed, and of all the

harsh things which ungodly sinners

have spoken against Him." Quoted

in Jude 14-15

IN THE BIBLE, THERE are few scriptures that talks about Archangel Michael. Here are scriptures reference for Michael:

Daniel 10:13: *"But the prince of the kingdom of Persia withstood me one and twenty days: but, lo, Michael, one of the chief princes, came to help me; and I remained there with the kings of Persia."*

Daniel 10:21: *"But I will shew thee that which is noted in the scripture of truth: and there is none that holdeth with me in these things, but Michael your prince."*

Daniel 12:1: *"And at that time shall Michael stand up, the great prince which standeth for the children of thy people: and there shall be a time of trouble, such as never was since there was a nation even to that same time: and at that time thy people shall be delivered, every one that shall be found written in the book."*

Jude 1:9: *"Yet Michael the archangel, when contending with the devil he disputed about the body of Moses, durst not bring against him a railing accusation, but said, The Lord rebuke thee."*

Revelation 12:7-9 (NIV): *"Then war broke out in heaven. Michael and his angels fought against the dragon, and the dragon and his angels fought back. But he was not strong enough, and they lost their place in heaven. The great dragon was hurled down—that ancient serpent called the devil, or Satan, who leads the whole world astray. He was hurled to the earth, and his angels with him."*

There are other scriptures that don't explicitly talk about Archangel Michael but still reference him. He has been in the game for so long—fighting the battle of the Lord as He is the heavenly leader of the Host of God. I strongly believe that every prophet of the bible we ever had, has also encountered Michael as the defender.

And we usually limit his character only to warfare. But there is more to Him. You will be surprised that even Gabriel who usually receives a message from the throne of God once influenced the Nephilim to fight each other during the time of Noah.

This is what the Book of Enoch had to say:

9The Lord said to Gabriel, "Proceed

against the bastards, the reprobates,

against the children of

fornication. [xxviii] Destroy the children

of fornication and the children of the

Watchers from amongst men. Cause them

to go forth against one another that they

may destroy each other in battle, for they

will not have long life.

10Grant no request that their fathers may make to

you on behalf of their children; for they

hope to live an eternal life; but none of

them will live past five hundred

years[xxix]."

This is the commission of Michael after the corruption of fallen angels and their offspring—Nephilim's. From the scripture below from the book of Enoch, Archangel Michael has to fight destruction and restore peace and righteousness to earth,

11The Lord said to Michael, "Go, tell

Semyaza and his associates who have

defiled themselves by marrying women,
that they and all those they contaminated
will be destroyed. 12When they have
seen their sons slay one another and all
their loved ones destroyed, bind them
for seventy generations[xxx] under the
valleys of the earth, until the day of their
judgment and of their end, till their last
judgment be passed for all eternity. 13In
those days they will be led off to the
fiery abyss, to the torment and the prison
in which they will be confined forever.
And 14whosoever was condemned and
destroyed will from thenceforth be
bound together with them to the end of
all generations.[xxxi] 15Destroy all the
spirits of the reprobate and the children
of the Watchers, because they have
oppressed mankind. 16Destroy all wrong

from the face of the earth and let every

evil work come to an end:

Angel Michael performs the will of God. The will of God is that we may live and have abundancy in all things. Thus after the destruction of the flood, God restored all things, blessings upon blessings came forth.

20Cleanse the earth from

all oppression, unrighteousness, sin,

godlessness, and all the uncleanness that

is wrought upon the earth destroy from

off the earth. 21Then all the children of

men will become righteous, and all

nations will worship Me, and will

praise Me, and all will worship Me.

Spiritual warfare

All men ought to fight the good fight of faith. All women too. If you want the generation to take the kingdom of God and run with it, they have to know about spiritual warfare. It has always been about the battle till you reach your destiny. Even the celestial bodies fight warfare against the evil powers restricting them over covering and protecting nations.

Occult and Satanic agents knows about the mystery of territory. If the city raises up godly altars, Holy Angels of God will mark it as their territorial space. Same applies when men and women sacrifices to demons—satanic stronghold will take its stand We have different levels of spiritual fight.

We are authorized to cast away demons. We also have legal authority as the church to bind and loose. Binding and loosing with the strategic mindset that the battle is in the air. Principalities and powers of darkness have thrones in the high places.

Ephesians 1:3 Blessed be the God and Father of our Lord Jesus Christ, who hath blessed

us with all spiritual blessings in heavenly places in Christ:

The spiritual blessings of God are for times like this. God the Father places all His children in Christ who dwells on high, far above principalities and powers of darkness. The greatest authority comes with the idea that we are seated in third heaven in the highest of the heavens. While the kingdom of the enemy is below. Through revelation and intense study of the Word of God, I have come to the conclusion that the kingdom of Satan is in the second heaven.

We all know about the famous story in Daniel 10 where Angel Gabriel was held captive by the Prince of Persia. Who ever thought of a Mighty Angel can be caged? And it did happen. But Michael, the prince, came to the rescue and fought against the kingdom of darkness.

The Prince of Persia and Prince of Greece are principalities in spirit. I would say fallen Angels who made a vow on Mount Hermon to go and indulge themselves with women.

Genesis 6: 1-4 And it came to pass, when men began to multiply on the face of the earth,

and daughters were born unto them,

2 That the sons of God saw the daughters of men that they were fair; and

they took them wives of all which they chose.

3 And the LORD said, My spirit shall not always strive with man, for that

he also is flesh: yet his days shall be an hundred and twenty years.

4 There were giants in the earth in those days; and also after that, when the sons of God came in unto the daughters of men, and they bare children to them,

the same became mighty men which were of old, men of renown.

Here is what Enoch had to say about the watchers—the Holy one who descended from heaven entrusted by God to watch over humanity. Nonetheless, they went on to mate with them, taking the form of human being while being Angels themselves.

The descended of 200 Angels (Book of Enoch 6-16)

It came to pass in those days that the

children of men multiplied and beautiful

and fair daughters[xi] were born unto

the m. 2The angels, the sons of the

heaven, saw and lusted after them, and

said to one another, "Come, let us

choose wives from among the children

of men and beget children." 3And their

leader, Semyaza, said to them, "I am

afraid that you will not truly agree to do

this deed, and I alone will have to pay

the penalty of this great sin." 4They all

answered him saying, "We should all swear to bind ourselves by a mutual oath not to abandon this plan, but to do this thi ng." 5So all together they bound themselves by an oath. There were two hundred, total, that descended[xii] in the days of Jared[xiii] upon Ardis, the summit of Mount Hermon.[xiv] 6They called it Mount Hermon, because they had sworn and bound themselves by oath upon it. 7These are the names of their leaders: Semyaza, their leader, Arakibal, Rameel, Akibeel, Tamiel, Ramuel, Danel, Ezeqeel, Barakel, Asael, Armaros, Batraal, Ananel, Zavebe, Samsapeel, Satarel, Turel, Yomyael, Sariel. 8These leaders led the rest of the two hundred angels.[xv]

I find it fit to include these story because hell broke after those incidents. Nephilim's came from hybrid of sexual encounter between women and Angels. Who later they disembodied souls became evil spirit of torment, affliction and corruption upon humanity. This is the battle every believer and non-believer is fighting whether we like it or not.

The fallen Ones went on to be the enemy of humanity. Manipulating and deceiving the chosen of God to miss heaven. The main aim of the kingdom of Satan is to turn man away from God.

By free will Lucifer decided to turn away from God and follow his own counsel.

Isaiah 14:12-16 How art thou fallen from heaven, O Lucifer, son of the morning! how art

thou cut down to the ground, which didst weaken the nations!

13 For thou hast said in thine heart, I will ascend into heaven, I will exalt

my throne above the stars of God: I will sit also upon the mount of the

congregation, in the sides of the north: 14 I will ascend above the heights of the

clouds; I will be like the most High.

15 Yet thou shalt be brought down to hell, to the sides of the pit.

16 They that see thee shall narrowly look upon thee, and consider thee,

saying, Is this the man that made the earth to tremble, that did shake kingdoms;

Ezekiel 28:13-19 Thou hast been in Eden the garden of God; every precious stone was thy

covering, the sardius, topaz, and the diamond, the beryl, the onyx, and the jasper,

the sapphire, the emerald, and the carbuncle, and gold: the workmanship of thy

tabrets and of thy pipes was prepared in thee in the day that thou wast created.

14 Thou art the anointed cherub that covereth; and I have set thee so: thou

wast upon the holy mountain of God; thou hast walked up and down in the midst

of the stones of fire.

15 Thou wast perfect in thy ways from the day that thou wast created, till

iniquity was found in thee.

16 By the multitude of thy merchandise they have filled the midst of thee

with violence, and thou hast sinned: therefore I will cast thee as profane out of

the mountain of God: and I will destroy thee, O covering cherub, from the midst

of the stones of fire.

17 Thine heart was lifted up because of thy beauty, thou hast corrupted thy

wisdom by reason of thy brightness: I will cast thee to the ground, I will lay thee

before kings, that they may behold thee.

18 Thou hast defiled thy sanctuaries by the multitude of thine iniquities, by

the iniquity of thy traffick; therefore will I bring forth a fire from the midst of

thee, it shall devour thee, and I will bring thee to ashes upon the earth in the

sight of all them that behold thee.

19 All they that know thee among the people shall be astonished at thee:

thou shalt be a terror, and never shalt thou be any more.

THESE SCRIPTURES ARE very important for believers to know about the cause of the fall of Lucifer—the anointed Cherubim. He is the only Cherubim named anointed in the bible. The show how honorable and influence he had in the heavenly realm. Cherubim are close to God. There are level of rank among Angels, and the closer you are to God, the more influence and glory you have. Since you are adorned by his countenance. I am not implying that some Angels are more powerful than others, I am talking about the glory of God.

The more you spend quality time in the secret place with The Most High, the more glorious you will be. Remember that Moses after talking to God, he was shining like an Angel. The secret of being filled with the goodness and the beauty of the Lord is to spend time with him.

We always talk about some "Me time" or some quality time. Spend your quality time with God. You will never regret every minute of it, even in the times to come. Many who have left this world, wish they could return once again and work for God. It is quite a blessing to serve the Most High God while in this land of the Living.

The perfect example is Jesus Christ—the son of the Living God. Even in His divinity, He pressed into the glory of God. He served His Father in all manner. And allowed the will of His Father to pass than His will. This is loyalty at its best.

We are in warfare; we are to submit ourselves under the will of God. As it is written, resist the devil, he shall flee from you. This is not a once off thing, we must deny our flesh daily. The flesh wage war with our spirit beings. The spirit must govern the body. Not the other way round.

There is therefore now no condemnation to them which are in Christ

Jesus, who walk not after the flesh, but after the Spirit.

2 For the law of the Spirit of life in Christ Jesus hath made me free from the

law of sin and death (Roman 8:1-2).

According to this scripture, it is the of spirit that shall quicken us. As God is spirit, so are we. And we are to walk in the same manner. He is Holy, therefore, we ought to be Holy. And it is the work of the Holy Spirit to empower faith people to walk in Holiness. I have come to conclusion that we will fall short if we are to self-righteous ourselves. Abraham was counted righteousness by God. Its God who is able to count us because of salvation He has put in place for us.

Salvation comes from God. He is the God of salvation and the God of righteousness.

Submit yourselves therefore to God. Resist the devil, and he will flee from

you.

8 Draw nigh to God, and he will draw nigh to you. Cleanse your hands, ye

sinners; and purify your hearts, ye double minded (James 4:7).

This is the ready for warfare; resist the devil. You cannot bind the devil, you can only bind demons. Therefore, resisting him is the only solution. By drawing near to God, by knowing who we are in Christ, by studying the Word of God and living according to faith. Faith quenches all the fiery darts of the enemy. Faith is our shield. The Word is the sword of the spirit.

12 For the word of God is quick, and powerful, and sharper than any

twoedged sword, piercing even to the dividing asunder of soul and spirit, and of

the joints and marrow, and is a discerner of the thoughts and intents of the heart (Hebrew 4:12).

Ministry of Michael

Hebrews 1:14 Are they not all ministering spirits, sent forth to minister for them who

shall be heirs of salvation?

Angels of God are ministering spirits who minister unto those who are heirs of salvation. Angels do not wish anyone to be lost. They celebrate the lost and found in the house of the Lord. It pleases them to lead the people of God to the salvation of their souls and eventually lead them to the eternal home of glory where God dwells.

Angels are mentioned 273 times throughout the Old and New Testaments, and other ancient-related records because God wants us to know their purpose. He created the angels to glorify Him and serve humanity on his behalf (as were we, Gen. 2).

Angels are spiritual beings above us temporarily until we reach Heaven. They are subject to Christ and they neither marry nor die and we are cautioned not to worship them. Angels are also called messengers, Watchers, military hosts, Sons of the Mighty, and Sons of God (I Peter 3: 22; Luke 20: 36; Matt. 22: 30; Rev. 4:8; Heb. 1: 16; Col. 2:18; Rev. 22: 8-9).

Archangel Michael is *the* supreme protector who guards against all effects of fear and fear-based energies. After all, this negative emotion is the driving force behind everything that's unsavory in this world. Without fear, we have peace. Michael will shield you from lower energies if you ask for his protection.

Hebrews 1:7 And of the angels he saith, Who maketh his angels spirits, and his

ministers a flame of fire.

The cool thing about spirits is that they don't need a visa to travel. They travel within a space and time in a blink of an eye. Since they are ministers of the flame of fire—they travel at a speed of life. It would take one a long time to descend from heaven, Angels travel at a supernatural speed. Many who had encounters with Angels, would very much agree that Angels talk in a mind-to-mind language, what we call telepathy.

I have had conversations with Angels in telepathic communication—thoughts to thoughts. It is not demonic since many Christians think it. This is one of the heavenly languages I have noticed through certain encounters.

God of the Heavens has blessed all His children with all spiritual gifts in the Heavenly places. Spirit of discernment is one of them. Through this gift, you can discern between spirits since some masquerade as the angels of light while not.

Let's dive into the ministry of Archangel Michael.

PROTECTION

"For He will give His angels charge concerning you, to guard you in all your ways."

Psalms 91:11 NASB

The word "Charge" means responsibility. He will give Angels the responsibility to safeguard you, protect you, bless you, and direct you into your calling in the Lord. Archangel Michael leads you, and guides in concerning all things that pertain to life. Especially your calling that requires attention; prophetic or Apostolic call. Men and women in high places, military leaders, officers, presidents, Ministers, etc. have a special place in the heart of Michael.

Michael is ready to serve and guide you in the name of the Lord. He is ever ready to step into your situation. As someone who has battled spiritual attacks from witches and wizards in my village, I have always seen Michael standing with me against evil forces. I would wake up at midnight to wage warfare in the spirit realm—charging the atmosphere with the fire of God.

In the spirit realm, I will see the mighty Angel standing guard to protect me against all the evil powers. When Angels are round, you sense the spirit of peace come on you, and all your fears are gone.

I have also seen the power of Psalm 91 at that time. It is a powerful prayer to date. When you are under the shadow of the Almighty God, you are invisible to the agents of the devil. They will look for you in spirit but will not succeed in finding you. Psalm 91 is the shelter of the servant of God.

Protect those who fear the Lord

As the defender of all that is pure, Michael is the epitome of strength and valor. He intervenes miraculously to save lives and to protect our bodies, loved ones, vehicles, belongings, and reputations.

Psalm 34:7 – the angel of the Lord encampeth around about them that fear him and keepeth them.

The fear of the Lord is the beginning of wisdom. When we fear the Lord, His covering upon us will never be broken. The Mighty Angels shall ascend and descend upon us with blessing, power, and honor. You are honored when you fear the Lord.

If you want to see the minister of the gospel of Christ ascending in glory, more and more, it can only be one thing—that is the fear of the Lord. The fear of the LORD comes with humility. God raises them up to those who walk in humility. Look at the Man of God Moses, he walked in perfect glory with God because of his humility.

You cannot think of humility and not think of Jesus Christ. Christ is the embodiment of humility. He is the embodiment of every gracious and pure word you can stretch your mind and think of. He is the Word Himself. If you meet this glorious being in His glorified body, you will run out of English terms to describe His glory and humility.

It came through revelation that Peter knew He was the Son of God. He was never on everyone's face about His divinity. He kept many of the miracles He wrought secretive.

1 Behold my servant, whom I uphold; mine elect, in whom my soul

delighteth; I have put my spirit upon him: he shall bring forth judgment to the

Gentiles.

2 He shall not cry, nor lift up, nor cause his voice to be heard in the street.

3 A bruised reed shall he not break, and the smoking flax shall he not

quench: he shall bring forth judgment unto truth.

4 He shall not fail nor be discouraged, till he have set judgment in the earth:

and the isles shall wait for his law. (Isaiah 42:1-4)

humility pays more than a billion dollars. Great influence and honor come with humility. God raises those. As we look at Archangel Michael, it was through that he said "Who is like God" when Lucifer rebelled from the Most High. It is from this question that he went on to challenge the morning star called Lucifer.

The name Michael means "Who is like God" as we have discussed earlier. He is loyal to God. He attended the voice of God, unlike Lucifer who wanted to do his own free will. Angels like Michael are the perfect example of what loyalty and humility mean.

Though, there are many who went astray because of pride—leading to rebellion. Even to this day, pride is the number one deadly weapon that destroys many lives. It was through pride that Lucifer fell. It was through pride that Eave was deceived. She wanted to be like God. She wanted God's status.

He gives direction

Acts 8:26 – Now an angel of the Lord spoke to Philip, saying arise and go toward the south along the road toward which goes down from Jerusalem to Gaza....and he arose and went

This is the directive command from the Angel 'arise and go'. God appears to us in different ways. He appeared to Philip through an Angel. He may not appear through you by an Angel but he will still pass His message through. He may speak to you through His Word, intuition, inner voice, dreams, visions and through prophetic people. Or even through signs.

He is the Living God. Though many may not see Angels literally, they are there. You will have to listen to your heart—your inner spirit, God can be found. As long as you are in Christ and indwelled by the Holy Spirit of God. When God speaks, we listen.

Prayer and fasting are the key that develops our spiritual eyes to harken to His voice. His voice is a small still voice that can only be heard when you all press in like Elijah. Elijah never gave up on a prayer while interceding for rain, he went and on, till the heavens gave away. It is the same attitude we should adorn ourselves with.

Apostles of Christ tarried in prayer and fasting. Consecrated themselves when they were about to send men and women on the mission. Apostle Paul is the product of intense prayer and fasting. Thus, he went on to be the greatest man in history for the kingdom of Christ. You will have to have a special relationship with the Living God to receive many revelations, understanding, wisdom, and knowledge he had. The fear of the Lord is the beginning of all great things. Brethren, fear the Living God.

Strengthen the call of God over your life

ACT27:23-24 – FOR THERE stood an angel by me this night an angel of God to whom I belong and serve.... saying 'Do not be afraid, Paul you must be brought before Caesar...

Angels are ministering spirits. They comfort us, support us, and care about our well-being. We will receive special attention from Angels when we walk in the purpose of God. God has assigned Angelic powers over your life to help out with your calling. Just like Jesus Christ who was strengthened by Angels when Satan was tempting Him. Satan did not only tempt Him while on the Mountain but throughout His ministry.

The Devil even though He was destroying Him was on the cross. Angel Michael was with Moses when he was commanded by God to deliver Israel out of Egypt. He strengthened Moses and fought the battle in the spirit realm against Egyptian principalities and powers of darkness. Every time there is spiritual warfare and physical warfare, Archangel Michael is there.

And come to think about it, you will always feel safe and protected when this being is around you. Michael is not just an ordinary Angel—he has a very special assignment to destroy the forces of darkness and chaining wandering stars that have rebelled against God. Satan will have it coming against Michael—this is the showdown unlike any other. he will arise in due time as we are approaching the end times.

We are blessed as the church of God because who are with us are mighty. If our eyes could be open like the eyes of Elisha, we shall see the wonder of God in the church. the Church of Jesus Christ is the church of authority and power against the kingdom of darkness.

STRENGTHENS YOUR FAITH

As we wage war in spirit with the enemy, it gets weary sometimes. From time to time, you will need cheering words that "You can do it". This is the work of the Holy Spirit—to empower us, inspire us and strengthen us in times like this. David strengthened Himself in the Lord. He knew where to go when in the pinnacle of death.

As the Lord is His shepherd, he would not want anything, and would not lack. Michael is here to strengthen your faith in the Lord. He will always point you to the Most High. So that you can experience no lack and every need met in your waking life.

Heaven is full of treasures and unclaimed blessings because of a lack of knowledge. One thing I have noticed that makes us fall short of the blessings of God is unscriptural prayers. God answers His own Word. His own Word is His Will. The will of God is revealed from Genesis to Revelation.

Strength is faith that will make it last through the journey. Many give up along the way. We have to keep the faith and keep going till we receive the very promises of God. Faith in God is having faith in His promises.

Faith comes through the Word. Faith is released through your mouth. Enlarge your mouth, eat the fruits of your labor.

Lead non-believers to repentance

Luke 15:7

"I tell you that in the same way, there will be more joy in heaven over one sinner who repents than over ninety-nine righteous persons who need no repentance."

Some people have entertained Angels without their knowledge. We do entertain them, sometimes we chase them away. I do not remember how many times I have come across people who have asked for money in town, some I will give them, some I will not. I remember this other day, this guy asked me for money to buy food, I thought he was just some random guy who was scamming me and I said "I don't have it". Then the was a sensation in my heart and a feeling of sorrow, I immediately turned back to give him, but he was not there. No more to be found. Within a blink of an eye, that guy was gone.

I have never felt so bad. You would never know, God works in a mysterious way. Again, I remember vividly this special moment, I have shared this story before. I was in a taxi going to a certain mall in town, then the driver lost his way on the road—heading in the opposite direction of the lane, then all of a sudden, I saw the heavens open in spirit, I saw the rides of the white horses coming to our aides. All I can remember is that no accident happened that day. It was all to the glory of the Most High.

Some of the things happen in the spirit realm. And it may not seem as if God is silent but He is working in the background. There have been numerous times in history when non-believers came to the Lord through Angels. And through the good gestures of Christian believers. Acts of goodness could save many. And can lead many to salvation. Mercy and compassion. Ministering with these virtues is the best gesture of the Holy Spirit. It is the work of the Holy Spirit to pull people but we are the vessels.

Michael shall arise

In the last chapter of the book of Daniel 12:1-4, it says Michael your prince shall arise. It talks about the end times—the great battle that shall follow between light and darkness. It is already happening to the extent that many elect are leaving their faith. There was a time in history when persecution was all-time high for believers in Christ.

This generation may not be experiencing physical persecution but spiritual persecution. Life is spiritual—and all things start in the spiritual reality before they manifest physically. The war that you see between Israel and Palestine, started in the spirit realm.

Adam was a spirit man before he was a physical being. God had already seen him before he created him. God is spirit and all those who serve Him must do so in spirit and in truth. We make the mistake of normally solving spiritual matter with physical matter. If you are somebody who neglects the life of the spirit, you will be short of glory many times, and shame will cover you.

As the body of Christ, faith and leading a healthy spiritual lifestyle is our number one goal. The man of sin is about to make a grand entrance into the world. Already the elites are preparing his entrance of destruction. This is the man who is the embodiment of Satan himself.

The game is that, as he is called the man of peace, the shall be destruction and war everywhere, and then he will make an appearance as the resolver of issues. This is someone with Satanic anointing but masquerades himself as an Angel of light. When they say "Peace, Peace, Peace" then destruction shall follow.

The elites and Mason know who this man is. Only the world and some Christian believers are unequivocal about him. There is always debate about who this man will come from which tribe and from which place he will come.

Our mission is to pray for the will of God to manifest in the world. And to pray for others in different walks of faith to come to Christ. To come to the real rock of our salvation. There is no salvation in any other name but in the name of Jesus Christ. Islam will not get you to experience the fullness of the glory of God, Christ will.

It is all about a relationship with God through his son.

1 Why do the heathen rage, and the people imagine a vain thing?

2 The kings of the earth set themselves, and the rulers take counsel together,

against the LORD, and against his anointed (Psalm 2:1-2).

As it happened during the time of David and Jesus Christ, we still see the movement of anti-God and anti-Christ. I have been in the religious in the past where I hardly heard the name of Jesus Christ preached. Mind you, it was a Christian church. where I am from, there are numerous Christian denominations where it is rare to hear the name of Jesus being exalted as the son of the Living God.

The name of the Lord is blasphemed from every corner. In music, in films, in art, and in overall—Christ is being persecuted once again. In the last days, people have become more and more anti-Christ, anti-Bible, and anti-God.

As someone who has studied Film and Television on a professional level, I see media being used as a weapon to distract men and women from God. Hollywood has caged many souls through their film industry agenda that glorifies Satan. Mind control is at an all-time high.

There has never been a time like this in history. We are the generation that is close to the second coming of Christ. However, it might not be in our time but it is in our timeline. As prophetic individuals, we have peaked in the spirit realm and have seen the preparation of the coming of the man of sin—anti-Christ.

There are many agents of Lucifer that are on the mission to foster this agenda to come to fullness. It is a sad reality because many political leaders of many nations have sold their people to the dark side for this satanic agenda. It is all about money, power, fame, and slavership of mankind.

I urge you brothers and sisters in the Lord to pray for the religion of Islam. We have billions of brothers and sisters who are lost. Not only them but to any party that does not see Christ as the Messiah of the new covenant of mankind to this day.

In the spirit realm, we see lost souls. Good people are lost because of a lack of knowledge and ignorance of the Word of Truth. Only truth shall set us free. Freedom is in the Lord God of our salvation—Christ Jesus.

It is not enough to know about Jesus Christ. But it is enough to walk in faith in the name of the Lord Jesus Christ, who is the way, truth, and life. Who does not want life? Who does not want life after death? It is he who does not want to do anything with the glorious One—Yeshua.

As much as we are preparing for the end times, the Angels are also on the move. As I am writing this book, I also considering doing a serious about this issue. Angelic powers are on the move for the end-time battle with the sons of darkness. Light and darkness have always been the enemy. It is light that diminishes darkness. It shall also be like that.

The veil is open. Christ's body was broken for our sake. The horses of heaven are coming. The sound of the chariot of battle is heard from a distance. Those with spiritually sensitive ears and eyes behold the wonders of God.

Take heart.

Working with angels

Archangels are God's most important messengers. As we have previously discussed, the word "archangel" means "chief angel," as the prefix arch means "chief," "principal," or "most important."

In the Bible, Michael is the only angel identified as an archangel (Jude 9). He is also called, "one of the chief princes" (Daniel 10:13), denoting his importance. Archangels are important angels who are actively involved in ensuring the well-being of every form of life on earth. Each archangel has a specific role to play in this.

Michael is always ready to protect, guide, and assist you in many different ways. Because they're so close to humanity, they're willing to help you in any way they can and will respond immediately to your call. You can ask them to help others, as well.

However, we do all things in the name of the Lord. You do not have authority to call them on your own, you call unto them in the name of the Lord. They listen to the voice of the Word of God. Therefore, it is important to be scriptural in prayer and under the direct will of God.

Archangels are tireless and can appear in more than one place at a time. You can call on any of the archangels for help and support whenever necessary in the name of the Lord, and be confident that they will instantly come to your aid.

God has charged all the Angel in your aid in times of trouble. As we are waging warfare, are Angels in spirit who paves the way for us. When we die, Angels come to us to present us before the Lord.

Shadrack, Meshach, and Abednego were preserved in the fire by the mighty Angel of God. Even though the Angel was not named, I believe, it was Archangel Michael who came to their rescue for their faith. Faith moves God, and God moves Angels at your rescue. Faith is important in our walk.

It is also through faith that you will work with the Angels of God. Desire spiritual gifts and you will be filled. The moment I heard these words, I started to press in more and more. The was a point in life where I desired the gift of the tongues, and I heard the small still voice say "It is through faith that you shall receive". Don't underestimate faith. We have a bunch of pastors submitting in her pastor's ministry for certain anointing. It is also through faith that you shall receive. Faith is still the pillar of the kingdom principles. God honors faith. I am talking about the action of faith that Abraham took. Take a first step like a child, the rest shall follow. Simple faith is the best response of every believer in every situation. Simple faith is "God got it all under control".

We acknowledge the Ancient of the days as the authority of everything going on in heaven, on earth, under the sea, underworld and in the world we cannot see with our physical eyes. Every activity in heaven revolve around the throne of the Most High God. Christ is the king. Angels very much submit under the authority of the Living God.

20 Bless the LORD, ye his angels, that excel in strength, that do his

commandments, hearkening unto the voice of his word (Psalm 103:20).

It is clear that Angels do not run errands at our own will but according to the will of the Father in the name of Jesus Christ. Since there are teachings that you can command legion of Angels at your disposal. Jesus Himself said "I can ask the Father to send legion of Angels on my behalf". So, it is as the Lord wishes but according to the proportion of our faith. As we have discussed, faith is the powerhouse of miracles, signs and wonder in this kingdom.

And also, be well versed with the ministry of the Word. You have to know the Word of God because they listen to the voice of His Word. His Word is the scriptures and promises in the Bible.

Prayers for Angelic Assistance

Let the Angels ascend and descend upon my life.

The Angel of the Lord support me

The Angel of the Lord minister unto me

The Angel of the Lord is charged over me to keep me in all my ways.

Oh Angel Michael arise in this season for my deliverance.

Oh Prince of God, Grant us peace in trying times.

Grant us peace of heart, mind, and soul in the name of the Lord.

Come Oh Michael in the name of the Lord and rebuke the deceiver.

Rebuke the manipulator in the name of Jesus.

Rebuke Satan for our sake in the name of the Lord.

Oh the Lord rebukes you, Satan.

Oh the Lord that guard against Jerusalem rebukes you, Devil!

Arise O the Host of the Army of the Heaven, executes divine judgment over principalities and powers of darkness.

Bind the prince of Persia from blocking our prayers in the name of Jesus Christ.

By the Word of the Lord, pave a righteous way for us in the name of Christ.

Michael the archangel of the Lord, persecute the enemy of my soul.

Michael the Angel of the Lord, fight for me in the heavens against principalities.

Save the Angel of the presence of God.

Make the crooked place straight in the name of Jesus.

Michael the Angel of the Lord, prosper me.

Michael the Angel of the Lord, deliver me from evil forces.

Send your Angels to mister to me O Lord.

I am an heir of salvation. Let the army of the heavenly minister the eternal Gospel of Christ unto me and my family.

Cover me with the light of your countenance Lord.

Meet me O Michael as I walk in my destiny in the name of the Lord.

Angelic Army of the Lord, fight for the church of Jesus Christ.

Send your Angel O Lord to reach for lost souls.

Send your Angels to smite demons that come to destroy me.

Angel of protection Prayer

Certainly! Here are 21 Angel of Protection prayers based on Psalm 91, designed to offer scriptural comfort and strength to someone seeking deliverance and protection from spiritual attacks:

1. Heavenly Father, I thank You for being my refuge and fortress, just as Psalm 91 proclaims. I ask for Your angel of protection to surround me and deliver me from all spiritual attacks.

2. Lord, I take refuge in Your shadow, and I trust in Your faithfulness. Send Your angels to guard and shield me from the enemy's schemes.

3. O God, I declare that You are my refuge, my fortress, and my God in whom I trust. Please deploy Your angels to protect me from every snare and trap.

4. I put my trust in Your promise that no evil will befall me. May Your angels watch over me and keep me safe from all harm.

5. Father, I claim the protection and deliverance promised in Psalm 91. Send Your angels to guard me in all my ways.

6. Lord, I take authority in the name of Jesus over every spiritual attack that comes against me. Send Your angels to fight on my behalf.

7. I declare that I dwell in the secret place of the Most High. May Your angels encamp around me and keep

me safe from harm.

8. Heavenly Father, I ask that Your angels bear me up, lest I strike my foot against a stone. Protect me from every stumbling block set by the enemy.

9. I trust in Your promise that I will tread upon the lion and the cobra. Send Your angels to give me dominion over every spiritual threat.

10. Lord, I believe in Your protection, and I rebuke every evil that seeks to harm me. Send Your angels to guard me from all harm and danger.

11. I declare that no plague shall come near my dwelling. May Your angels protect my home and family from all spiritual attacks.

12. Father, I take refuge in You, and I trust in Your angels to keep me safe from all harm and evil influences.

13. I stand on Your promise that I will not fear the terror by night. Send Your angels to watch over me and grant me peaceful sleep.

14. Lord, I rebuke every demonic force that comes against me. Send Your angels to fight the battles on my behalf.

15. I declare that I am under the watchful eye of Your angels day and night. Protect me from all spiritual attacks and schemes.

16. Heavenly Father, I thank You for the shield of Your angels that surrounds me. Keep me safe from all harm and danger.

17. I trust in Your faithfulness, O God, and I ask that Your angels deliver me from every spiritual snare and temptation.

18. I declare that I am under the divine protection of Your angels, and no weapon formed against me shall prosper.

19. Lord, I take refuge in Your name, and I trust in Your angels to keep me safe from all spiritual attacks and oppression.

20. Father, I rebuke every demonic presence that comes against me. Send Your angels to drive them away and grant me peace and deliverance.

21. I stand firm on Your promise in Psalm 91, and I thank You for Your angelic protection. Keep me safe, O Lord, and deliver me from all spiritual attacks. In Jesus' name, I pray. Amen.

These prayers are inspired by the protective and comforting words of Psalm 91 and can serve as a source of strength and encouragement for someone seeking deliverance and protection from spiritual attacks.

Angel Michael Prayer

Certainly! Here are 21 Angel Michael Protection prayers based on the themes of Psalm 35, designed to offer scriptural comfort and strength to someone seeking deliverance from spiritual attacks and invoking the protection of the archangel Michael:

1. Heavenly Father, I call upon the powerful intercession of Archangel Michael, the defender of the faithful, to protect me in my time of spiritual battle, just as David sought Your help in Psalm 35.
2. Archangel Michael, warrior of light, come to my aid and shield me from the attacks of the enemy, just as David cried out for protection from those who sought to harm him.
3. Lord, I invoke the protection of Archangel Michael, the angel of strength and courage, to stand with me and defend me against the spiritual foes that seek to oppress me.
4. Archangel Michael, I trust in your mighty sword and unwavering loyalty to God. Guard me from all spiritual adversaries as David sought deliverance from his enemies.
5. I declare that I am under the protection of Archangel Michael's powerful wings. Surround me with your heavenly forces, and let no harm come near me.
6. Archangel Michael, the great protector, I ask for your

intervention against all forces of darkness that assail me, just as David called for help against his enemies.

7. Lord, grant me the strength and courage to face the spiritual battles that rage around me, and send Archangel Michael to guide and protect me in my hour of need.

8. I take refuge in the powerful shield of Archangel Michael, trusting that his presence will shield me from the fiery darts of the enemy.

9. Archangel Michael, I invoke your intercession to defend me against the evil plots and attacks that surround me, just as David sought deliverance from those who conspired against him.

10. I declare that I am under the watchful eye of Archangel Michael, and I ask for his assistance in vanquishing all spiritual adversaries who come against me.

11. Archangel Michael, the guardian of souls, protect me from the spiritual snares and traps set by the adversary, just as David cried out for deliverance from the wicked.

12. Lord, I trust in your divine providence, and I invoke the powerful presence of Archangel Michael to safeguard me from all spiritual harm.

13. Archangel Michael, I call upon your strength and might to help me stand firm against the spiritual attacks that seek to harm my soul, just as David sought protection against his enemies.

14. I declare that I am under the heavenly banner of Archangel Michael, and I ask for his assistance in

driving away all spiritual oppression and darkness.

15. Archangel Michael, I trust in your unwavering commitment to God's will, and I seek your protection against all spiritual enemies that seek to harm me.

16. Lord, I ask that you send Archangel Michael to fight on my behalf against the spiritual adversaries that threaten my peace, just as David called upon you for help.

17. Archangel Michael, the leader of the heavenly armies, come to my aid and protect me from all forms of spiritual warfare, just as David sought deliverance from his foes.

18. I declare that I am under the guidance of Archangel Michael's sword and shield, and I ask for his protection against all spiritual attacks and oppression.

19. Archangel Michael, I trust in your authority and power, and I seek your assistance in defeating the spiritual forces that come against me, just as David sought protection from his enemies.

20. Lord, I take refuge in your mercy, and I ask that you send Archangel Michael to protect me and lead me to victory in my spiritual battles, just as David sought deliverance from his adversaries.

21. Archangel Michael, defender of the faithful, I place my trust in your protection and pray for your intercession in my time of need. Guard me from all spiritual harm and deliver me from the snares of the enemy.

These prayers are intended to invoke the protection and strength of Archangel Michael, a powerful figure in Christian tradition associated with spiritual warfare, and can serve as a source of solace and empowerment for someone facing spiritual attacks.

Deliverance through Psalms

Prayer for Protection (Based on Psalm 91): Heavenly Father, I come before You, seeking Your divine protection. Just as Psalm 91 assures us of Your shelter, I ask that Your wings cover me, and I dwell in Your secret place. Keep me safe from all harm, danger, and evil. Send Your angels to guard me and my loved ones day and night. I trust in Your promise of deliverance and protection, and I find refuge in You, my stronghold. In Jesus' name, I pray. Amen.

Prayer for Prosperity (Based on Psalm 121): Lord, as I journey through life, I look to You, the Maker of heaven and earth, for guidance and prosperity. Just as Psalm 121 tells us that our help comes from You, I ask for Your blessings on my endeavors. May my steps be ordered by You, and may I find success in all that I do. Keep me from all harm and watch over my going out and coming in. In Your name, I seek prosperity, and I trust in Your provision. Amen.

Prayer for Success (Based on Psalm 146): God, I praise You with all my being, just as Psalm 146 teaches us to put our trust in the Lord. I seek Your guidance and wisdom in all my endeavors. Grant me the ability to make wise choices and prosper in my work and relationships. Let everything I do be in alignment with Your will. I believe in Your power to grant me success and prosperity. In Jesus' name, I pray. Amen.

Prayer for Deliverance (Based on Psalm 21): Heavenly Father, I thank You for the victories and deliverance You provide, as we see in Psalm 21. I come before You seeking deliverance from all challenges and obstacles that stand in my way. Grant me the strength and courage to face them, knowing that You are my refuge and fortress. Just as You answered the psalmist's cry for help, I trust in Your deliverance and ask for Your guidance in every circumstance. In Jesus' name, I pray. Amen.

May these prayers provide you with the protection, prosperity, and success you seek, and may you find comfort and strength in the promises of these Psalms.

Notes

Archangels 101: How to connect closely with Archangels Michael, Raphael, Gabriel, Uriel, And Others For Healing, Protection And Guidance By Doreen Virtue.

https://www.jewishvirtuallibrary.org/azazel

Don't miss out!

Visit the website below and you can sign up to receive emails whenever Johannes Tefo publishes a new book. There's no charge and no obligation.

https://books2read.com/r/B-A-UEZX-CCNXC

Connecting independent readers to independent writers.

Did you love *Michael For Warfare*? Then you should read *The 24: Prophetic Word For This Season 2024 And Beyond*[1] by Johannes Tefo!

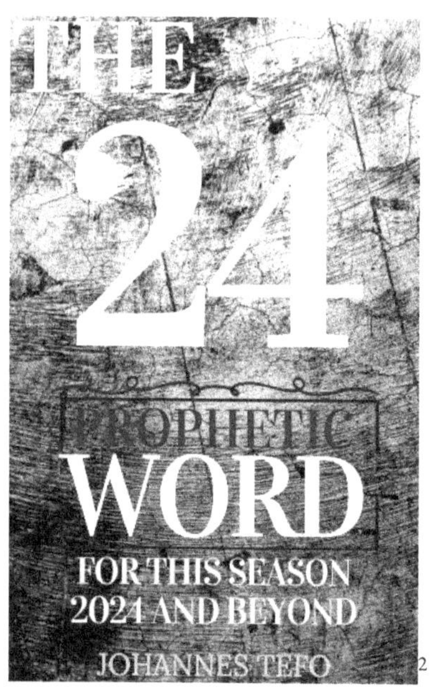

[2]

Embark on a transformative journey into the heart of divine revelation with "The 24: Prophetic Word For this Season 2024 and Beyond." In this awe-inspiring book, a celestial tapestry of prophetic insights unfolds, offering a roadmap for navigating the currents of 2024 and beyond. Authored with divine inspiration, this book unveils the intricate details of a profound message delivered by the Almighty.

---

1. https://books2read.com/u/3JLVaB

2. https://books2read.com/u/3JLVaB

Prepare to be captivated as the pages reveal twenty-four prophetic words, each a beacon of guidance for the faithful navigating the currents of our times. Immerse yourself in the sacred whispers of the Lord, offering solace and wisdom for the challenges and triumphs that lie ahead.

"The 24" is more than a book; it's a sacred dialogue, a conduit for divine messages that illuminate the path towards spiritual enlightenment and purpose. As you absorb the revelations within, anticipate a profound transformation in your faith and understanding of the divine plan.

This book is not merely a collection of words; it's a spiritual compass pointing towards hope, faith, and fulfillment in the seasons to come. Open its pages, embrace the prophetic wisdom, and step into a future illuminated by the divine light of "The 24." Your spiritual journey begins here.

Also by Johannes Tefo

Family spiritual Warfare Books

Generational Curses And Spiritual Warfare: Spiritual Strategies & Principles Of Victory Against Evil Strongholds

Youth's Guide To Spiritual Warfare

A Women's Guide To Spiritual Warfare

Standalone

Deliver Your Soul From Evil

Overcoming Spirit Of Stagnation

The 24: Prophetic Word For This Season 2024 And Beyond

Michael For Warfare

Territorial Spirits: Overcome Evil Strongholds in Your Life And Take Over Your Community With Strategic Warfare And Winning Prayers

Prayers Against Suicide Spirit

Spiritual Warfare When Enough is Enough

Identity In Christ

Prayers Against Satanic Networks

The Workplace You Need: Spiritual Warfare Prayers That Silence Evil Powers At Your Workplace.

Deliverance From Mind Control: Be Free And Delivered From Every Marine Demons Of Mind Control

Times Getting Hard: Scriptures Of Comfort For Hard Days

Battle In The Sea: How To Tackle Spiritual Warfare And Win The Battle

Freedom: Deliverance Of Souls From Captivity

A Dedicated Prayer Lifestyle: Simple Tips To Effective Prayer Lifestyle

Deliverance From Sexual Dreams

Sexual Lust, Demons, And Impurity

Redefined By Fire: Unleashing The Power Of The Holy Spirit Within.

About the Author

Before he started writing Christian books, Johannes got a graduate degree in Film and Television from university of Johannesburg. After that, just to shake things up, he went to equip himself with religious studies, particularly Christianity, just to have knack about the world beyond the curtains of time. And how this body of Christ has transformed millions of people around the world, not neglecting how sadly the movement has been persecuted from time to time. He now writes full time.